Praise for *I'm Like You, You're Like Me:*

A Parent Council® Selection

"A wonderful book for helping young children understand and appreciate people who are different from themselves while discovering and developing their own unique traits and skills."
—The National PTA's *Our Children* Magazine

"A marvelous celebration of tolerance and diversity."
—*All Together Now* Magazine

I'm Like You, You're Like Me

A Child's Book About Understanding and Celebrating Each Other

By Cindy Gainer

free spirit PUBLiSHiNG® Works for kids®

Printed in Hong Kong

Library of Congress Cataloging-in-Publication Data

Gainer, Cindy.
     I'm like you, you're like me: a child's book about understanding and celebrating each other / by Cindy Gainer.
          p.   cm.
     Summary: Illustrations and simple text explore ways in which children are alike and some ways they may be different.
     ISBN 1-57542-039-2
     1. Individual differences in children--Juvenile literature. [1. Individuality.] I. Title.
     BF723.I56G35   1998

                                                 98-27671
                                                   CIP

Book design by Marieka Heinlen
Printing and binding by Paramount Printing Company Limited
The illustrations are done in pen and marker on posterboard.

10 9 8 7 6 5 4

Free Spirit Publishing Inc.
217 Fifth Avenue North, Suite 200
Minneapolis, MN 55401-1299
(612) 338-2068
help4kids@freespirit.com
www.freespirit.com

Printed in Hong Kong

To Bill and August, who share my life.
It is my blessing to share in theirs.

And to William A. Sorrels, M.Ed.,
for his invaluable knowledge and encouragement.

You and I are alike in many ways.

We may be the same age
or live on the same street.

We may go to the same school
or even have the same name.

We are different from each other, too.

Our hair may be brown or blond or red or black.

Our eyes may be blue or brown or green.

Our skin may be dark or light or in between.

It's fun to find ways I'm like you
and you're like me.

It's fun to find ways we're different.

One of us is bigger,
and the other is smaller.

One of us has curly hair,
the other has straight hair.

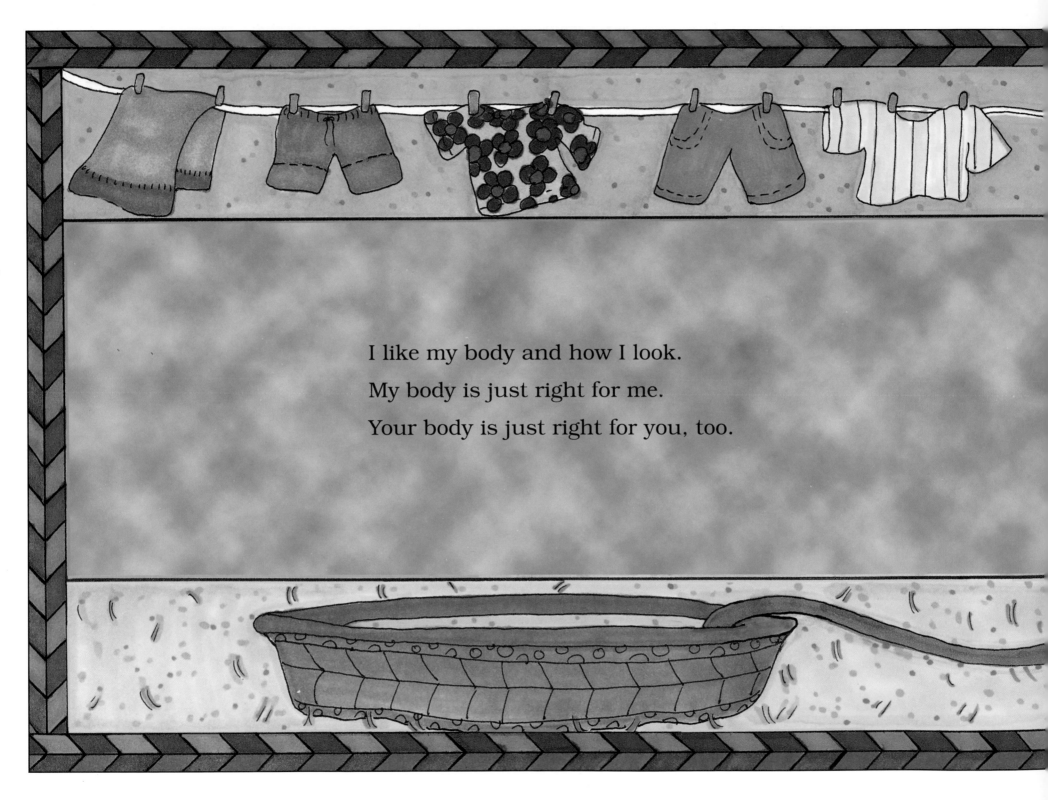

I like my body and how I look.

My body is just right for me.

Your body is just right for you, too.

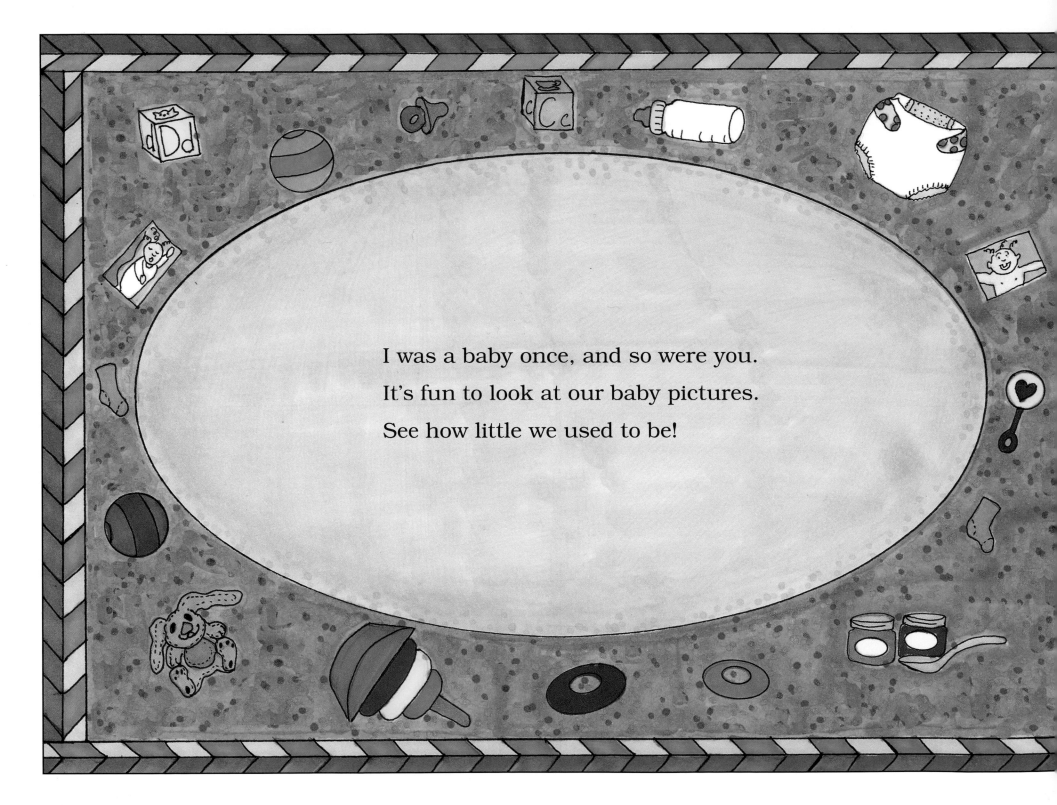

I was a baby once, and so were you.

It's fun to look at our baby pictures.

See how little we used to be!

I've learned how to do
some things by myself,
and so have you.

We can both tie our shoes.

We can both ride a bike.

We can both write our names.

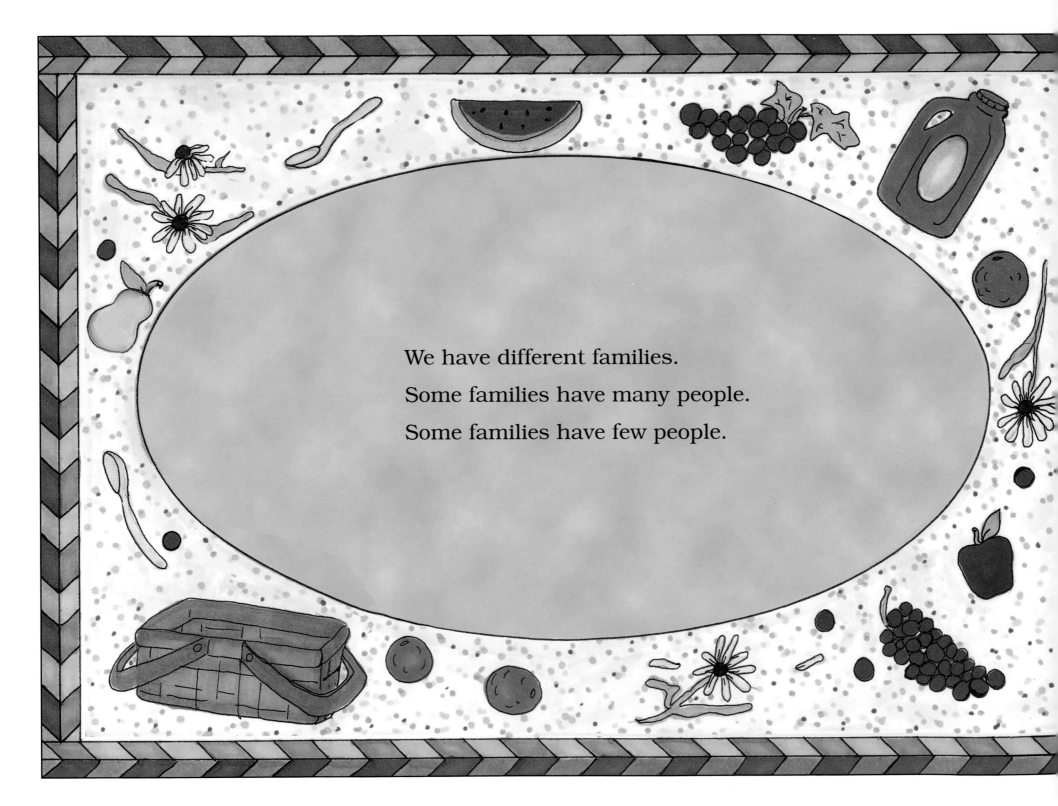

We have different families.

Some families have many people.

Some families have few people.

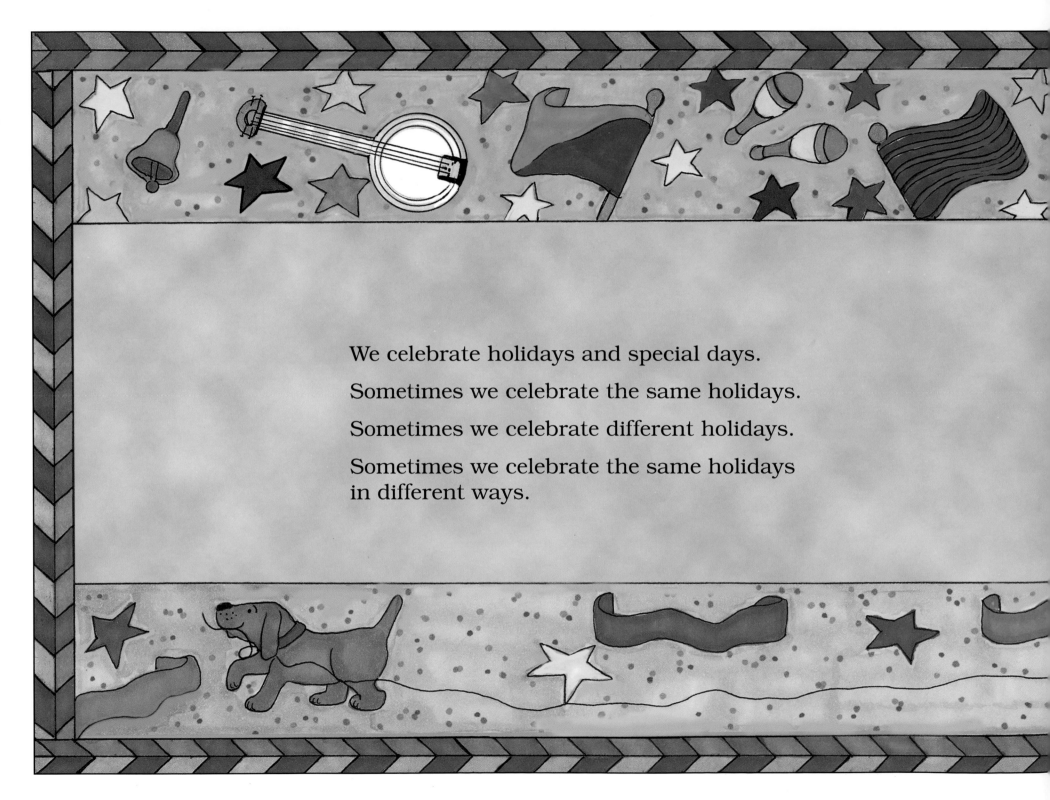

We celebrate holidays and special days.

Sometimes we celebrate the same holidays.

Sometimes we celebrate different holidays.

Sometimes we celebrate the same holidays in different ways.

Even though we're different in some ways,
we can enjoy being together.

We can show that we like
and welcome each other.

We can learn to accept each other.

I feel accepted when you invite me
to your home to play.

Or when you want to be my buddy
as we line up for playground time.

I feel accepted when you say
I'm your friend.

We can listen to each other.

This is a good way to get to know each other better.

We can learn more ways we're alike and different.

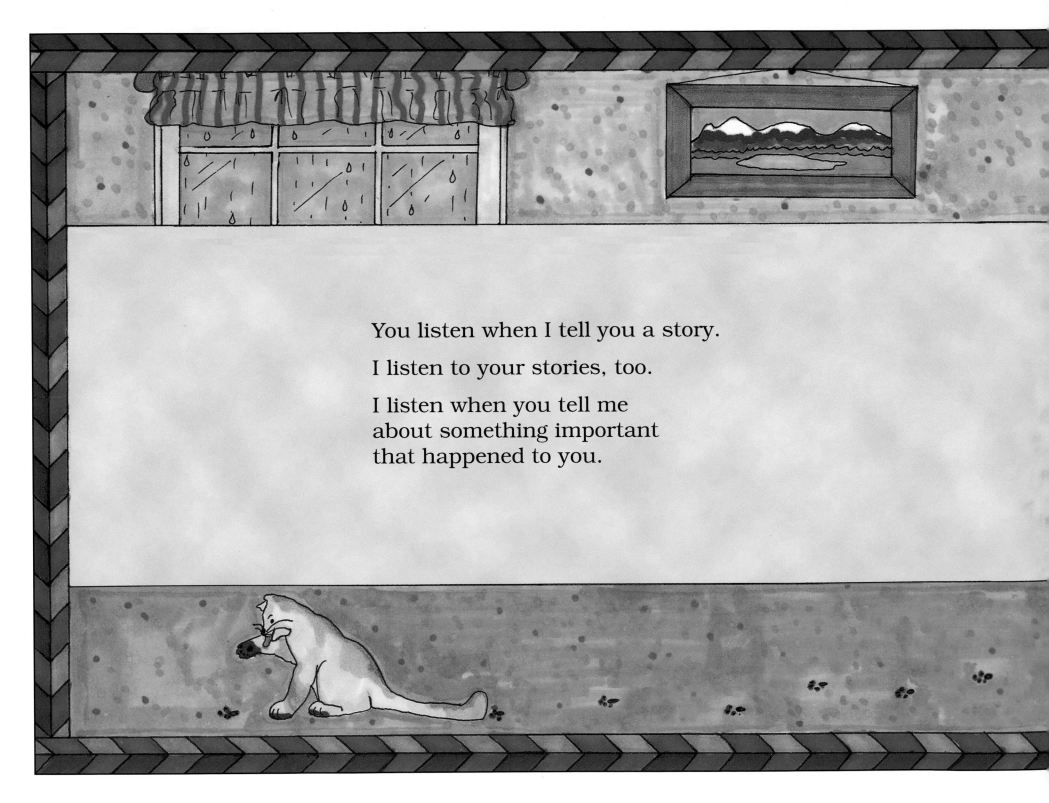

You listen when I tell you a story.

I listen to your stories, too.

I listen when you tell me
about something important
that happened to you.

We can tell each other
about things we like
and things we don't like.

We can try our best
to understand each other.

I can tell you how I'm feeling.

You can tell me how you're feeling, too.

We can tell each other what we want
and what we need.

Sometimes we want the same things.

Sometimes we want different things.

We can try our best to be kind to each other.

Even when we don't agree with each other.

Even when we feel tired or upset.

It's unkind to make fun of each other
or call each other names.

This is how feelings get hurt.

Let's be nice instead.

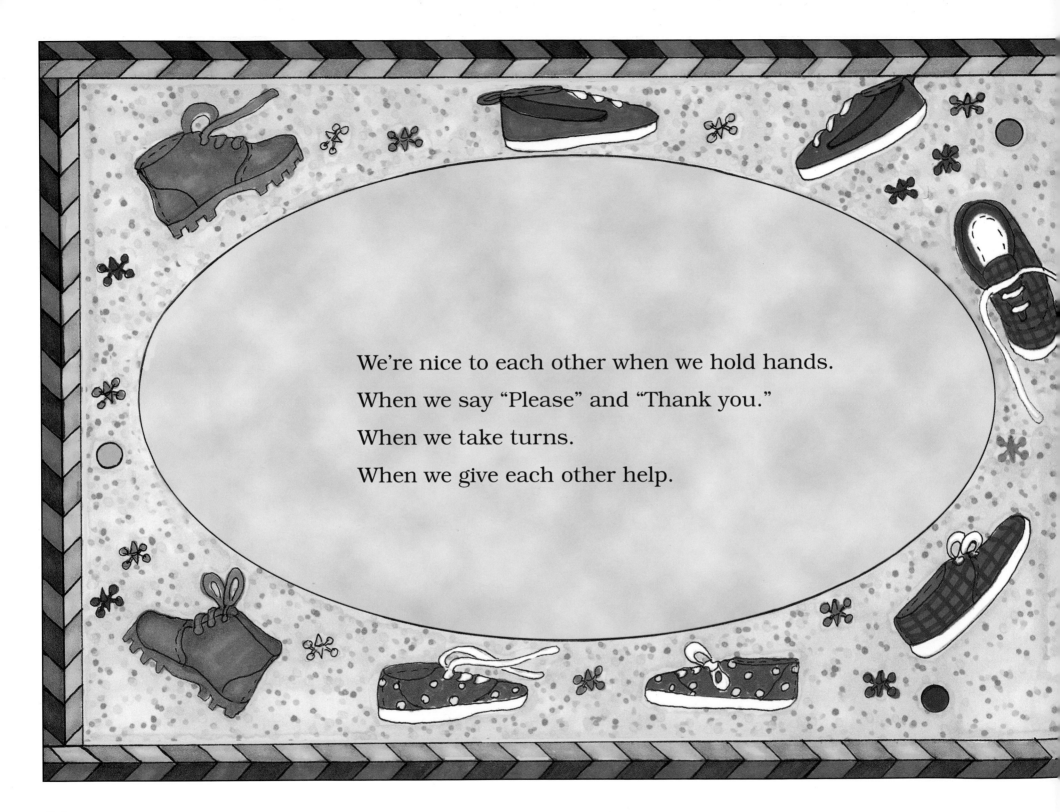

We're nice to each other when we hold hands.

When we say "Please" and "Thank you."

When we take turns.

When we give each other help.

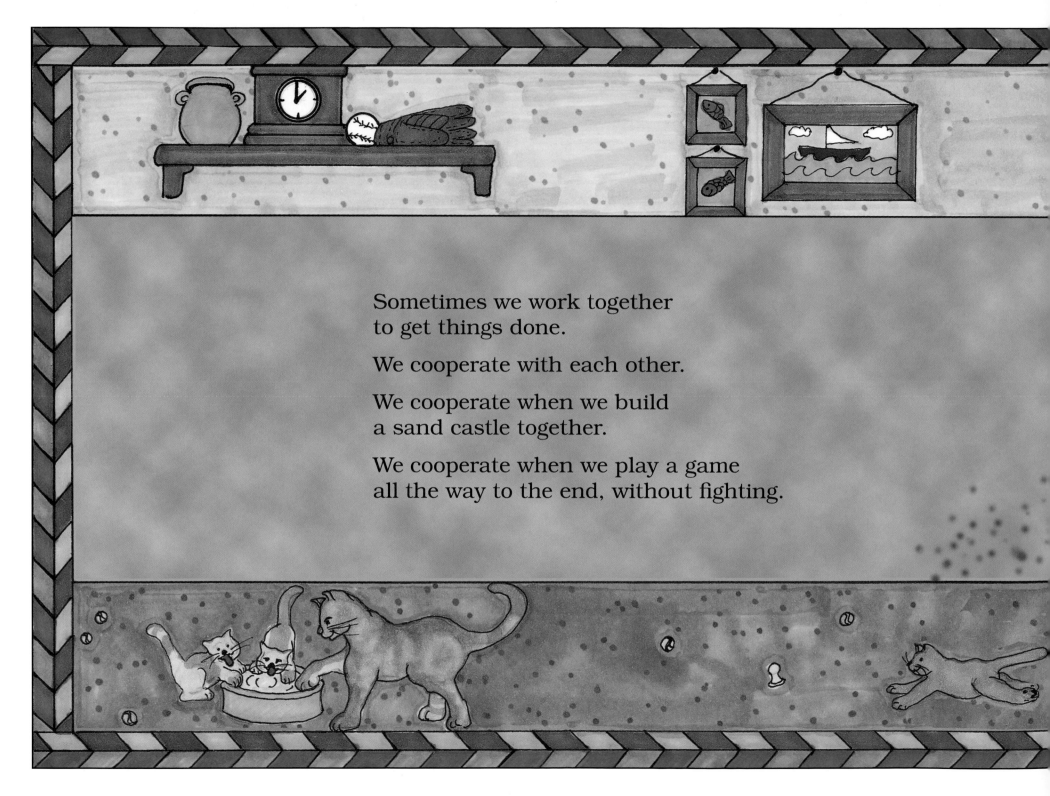

Sometimes we work together
to get things done.

We cooperate with each other.

We cooperate when we build
a sand castle together.

We cooperate when we play a game
all the way to the end, without fighting.

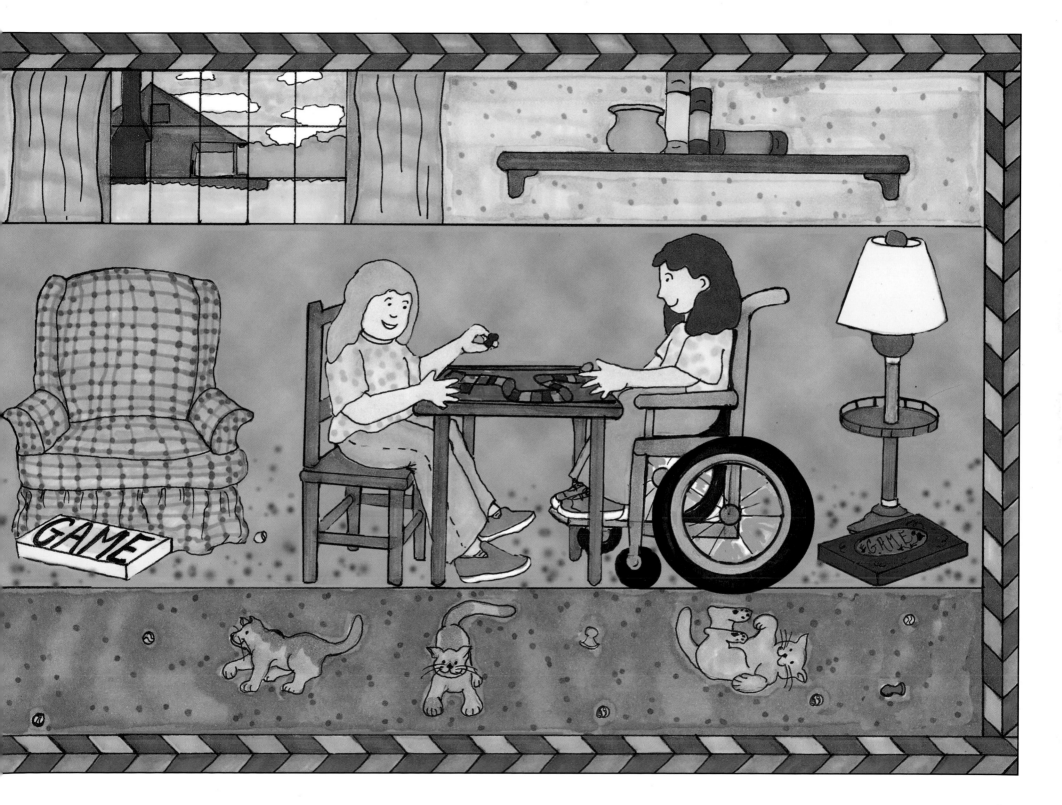

When we cooperate,
we can do almost anything!

We can play together
and work together.

We can be friends.

I'm like you, you're like me.

But we're not exactly the same.

That's why I like you
and you like me.

41

Cindy Gainer has a B.F.A. with Early Childhood and Art Education Certification from Seton Hill College in Greensburg, Pennsylvania, and is currently participating in the Gestalt Training for Professionals Program in Pittsburgh. She is the coauthor and illustrator of the award-winning books *Good Earth Art: Environmental Art for Kids* (Bright Ring Publishing) and *MathArts: Exploring Math through Art for 3 to 6 Year Olds* (Gryphon House). She has taught art to children from grades kindergarten through 12 in Pennsylvania schools, appeared on television, and has given numerous workshops to teachers and students as an author/illustrator. Cindy owns Little Red Schoolhouse, a preschool for four- and five-year-olds, where she is actively involved in teaching young learners and fostering positive child development. Cindy resides in Jeannette, Pennsylvania, with her husband, Bill Matrisch, and their son, August.

Also by the author: *A Leader's Guide to I'm Like You, You're Like Me*, a companion to the children's book

OTHER GREAT BOOKS FROM FREE SPIRIT

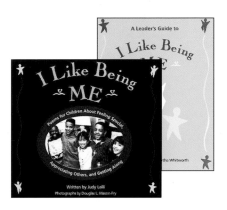

Just Because I Am
A Child's Book of Affirmation
*by Lauren Murphy Payne, M.S.W.,
illustrated by Claudia Rohling*

"I am a person. I am special. I am
important … just because I am."
Warm, simple words and enchanting
illustrations strengthen and support
young children's self-esteem.
For ages 3–8.
32 pp., color illust., softcover, 7⅝" x
9¼", ISBN 0-915793-60-1, $8.95

A Leader's Guide to
Just Because I Am
*by Lauren Murphy Payne, M.S.W.,
illustrated by Claudia Rohling*

Thirteen lessons reinforce the
messages of the child's book.
Includes activities, questions,
and reproducible Home Handouts
for parents.
Preschool through grade 3.
56 pp., illust., softcover, 8½" x 11",
ISBN 0-915793-61-X, $13.95

We Can Get Along
A Child's Book of Choices
*by Lauren Murphy Payne, M.S.W.,
illustrated by Claudia Rohling*

Simple words and inviting
illustrations teach children how
to get along with others and resolve
conflicts peacefully.
For ages 3–8.
36 pp., color illust., softcover, 7⅝" x
9¼", ISBN 1-57542-013-9, $9.95

A Leader's Guide to
We Can Get Along
*by Lauren Murphy Payne, M.S.W.,
illustrated by Claudia Rohling*

Fifteen lessons reinforce the
messages of the child's book.
Includes activities, questions,
and reproducible Home Handouts
for parents.
Preschool through grade 3.
64 pp., illust., softcover, 8½" x 11",
ISBN 1-57542-014-7, $14.95

I Like Being Me
Poems for Children About Feeling
Special, Appreciating Others, and
Getting Along
*by Judy Lalli
photographs by Douglas L. Mason-Fry*

Rhyming poems and black and white
photographs explore issues important
to young children—being kind, solving
problems, and more.
For ages 3–8.
64 pp., photos, softcover, 8¼" x 7¼",
ISBN 1-57542-025-2, $9.95

A Leader's Guide to
I Like Being Me
*by Judy Lalli
and Mary Martha Whitworth*

Twenty-six lessons reinforce the
messages of the child's book.
Includes activities, questions,
and reproducible Home Handouts
for parents.
Preschool through grade 3.
80 pp., illust., softcover, 8½" x 11",
ISBN 1-57542-026-0, $16.95

A Leader's Guide to
I'm Like You, You're Like Me
A Child's Book About Understanding
and Celebrating Each Other
by Cindy Gainer

Twenty lessons reinforce the
messages of the child's book.
Includes activities, questions,
and reproducible Home Handouts
for parents.
Preschool through grade 3.
80 pp., illust., softcover, 8½" x 11",
ISBN 0-915793-61-X, $16.95

*To place an order or to request a free
catalog of materials, please write,
call, email, or visit our Web site:*

Free Spirit Publishing Inc.
217 Fifth Avenue North • Suite 200
Minneapolis, MN 55401-1299
call toll-free 800.735.7323
or locally 612.338.2068
fax 612.337.5050
help4kids@freespirit.com
www.freespirit.com

Visit us on the Web!
www.freespirit.com

Stop by anytime to find our Parents' Choice Approved catalog with fast, easy, secure 24-hour online ordering; "Ask Our Authors," where visitors ask questions—and authors give answers—on topics important to children, teens, parents, teachers, and others who care about kids; links to other Web sites we know and recommend; fun stuff for everyone, including quick tips and strategies from our books; and much more! Plus our site is completely searchable so you can find what you need in a hurry. Stop in and let us know what you think!

Just point and click!

new! Get the first look at our books, catch the latest news from Free Spirit, and check out our site's newest features.

contact Do you have a question for us or for one of our authors? Send us an email. Whenever possible, you'll receive a response within 48 hours.

order! Order in confidence! Our secure server uses the most sophisticated online ordering technology available. And ordering online is just one of the ways to purchase our books: you can also order by phone, fax, or regular mail. No matter which method you choose, excellent service is our ultimate goal.

Win free books! As a way of thanking everyone who's made our Web site a success, we often have book giveaways online. Stop by and get in on the action!